Ashley
McCruden

Picture credits:
l: Left, r: Right, t: Top, b: Bottom, c: Centre

Front Cover Images: tl : NASA, tr: NASA, ml: Al Rublinetsky/ Shutterstock,
b: Natalia Bratslavsky/ Istockphoto,
Back Cover Images: tl: NASA, ml: Aristide Bergamasco/ Shutterstock, b: Andrey Ushakov/ Shutterstock.
Border Images: NASA, Pichugin Dmitry/ Shutterstock, Terry Chan/ Shutterstock,
J. Helgason/ Shutterstock.

Inside: 6t : NASA, 6b: NASA, 7t: NASA, 7b: NASA, 8t: NASA/ ESA, 8b: NASA, 9t: NASA/ ESA, 9b: NASA/ ESA,
10t: NASA/ ESA, 10b: NASA, 11t: NASA/ ESA, 11b: NASA, 12m: NASA, 13t: NASA/ ESA, 13m : NASA/ ESA,
14b: Pichugin Dmitry/ Shutterstock, 15t: NASA, 15m: NASA, 15b: NASA, 17t: NASA,
17b: Willem Bosman/ Shutterstock, 18t: Juerg Schreiter/ Shutterstock, 18b: Dainis Derics/ Shutterstock,
19: Pichugin Dmitry/ Shutterstock, 21: Gumenuk Vitalij/ Dreamstime, 22t: USGS, 22br: USGS,
25t: Andrea Hornackova/ Dreamstime, 26t: Natalia Bratslavsky/ Istockphoto, 26b: Martine Oger/ Shutterstock, 27: Aristide
Bergamasco/ Shutterstock, 29b: Vinicius Tupinamba/ Shutterstock,
30b: Vladimir Melnik/ Shutterstock, 31: José Carlos Pires Pereira/ Istockphoto, 32t: Laurin Rinder/ Dreamstime, 32b: Colin & Linda
McKie/ Shutterstock, 33t: Amlet/ Shutterstock, 33b: Dan Eckert/ Istockphoto,
34: Johnny Lye/ Istockphoto, 35t: Vera Bogaerts/ Shutterstock, 35b : Tomasz Szymanski/ Shutterstock,
36t : Iofoto/ Shutterstock, 36b : Andrey Ushakov/ Shutterstock, 37t: David Mckee/ Shutterstock,
37b: Mario Savoia/ Shutterstock, 38t: Efremova Irina/ Shutterstock, 38b: Sven Klaschik/ Istockphoto,
39b: Gianluca Figliola Fantini/ Shutterstock, 40t: Kulemza Maxim & Krasheninnikova Alina/ Shutterstock,
40b: Armen Eremyan/ Dreamstime, 41: YinYang/ Shutterstock, 42: Jon Bratt.

Published By Robert Frederick Ltd.
4 North Parade, Bath, BA1 1LF, England

First Published: 2008

NATURAL WORLD

CONTENTS

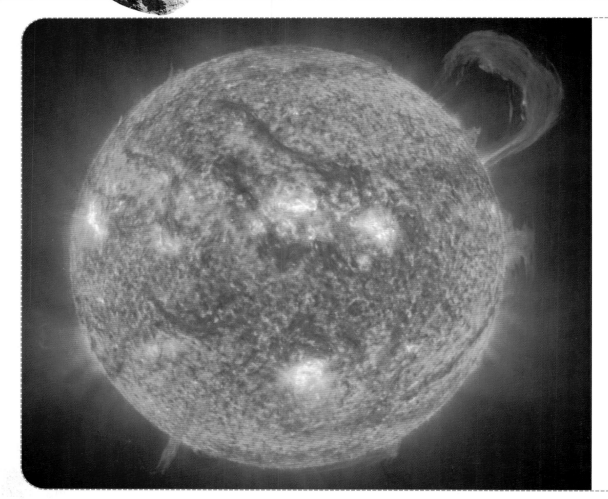

HOTTEST POINT ON THE SUN

The Sun is like a huge ball of fire. But did you know that temperatures on different parts of the Sun vary quite dramatically? The centre of the Sun, invisible to the naked eye, is called the core. This is actually the hottest part of the Sun at around 13.6 million Kelvin (13.6 million degrees Celsius or 24.4 million degrees Fahrenheit)!

COOLEST LAYER ON THE SUN

The surface of the Sun has a temperature of about 5,800 Kelvin (5,526 degrees Celsius or 10,000 degrees Fahrenheit), which is lower than any other part. This makes it the coolest part of the Sun. The Sun is made up of layers of gases. The layer around the Sun, about 311 miles (500 km) above the photosphere (the part of the Sun visible to us), is the coolest at about 4,000 Kelvin (3,727 degrees Celsius or 6,740 degrees Fahrenheit).

HIGHEST MOUNTAIN ON THE MOON

The moon has several mountain ranges and peaks. Mons Huygens, part of the Montes Apenninus range, is the highest mountain on the Moon. The 4,700 m- (15,420 ft-) high mountain is named after the Dutch mathematician and astronomer Christiaan Huygens (1629–1695), who patented the first pendulum clock. The Apollo 15 mission landed close to Mons Huygens on 30 July 1971. Mons Hadley is just a little shorter than Huygens at 4,600 m (15,091 ft) high.

HOTTEST LAYER OF THE SUN

The corona, or the outer portion of the Sun's atmosphere, is the hottest part of the Sun visible to the eye. It is about 2 million Kelvin (2 million degrees Celsius or 3.6 million degrees Fahrenheit). The corona is plasma that stretches more than a million kilometres around the Sun. This plasma emits X-rays. Solar wind also originates here. The corona is most visible during a solar eclipse, as pictured right.

DEEPEST CRATER ON THE MOON

Craters are the dents on the surface of the Moon caused by a collision with meteorites, comets or asteroids. Since the Moon has no atmosphere, there is nothing to protect it from these collisions. There are millions of craters on the moon, among which Newton is the deepest, dropping 8,839 m (29,000 ft). Newton is oblong in shape. The angle of impact has left one end narrow and flat and covered with lava, while the other end is wider and irregular. Other significant craters on the moon include Bailly, Casatus, Klaproth, Moretus and Short.

Did you know?

The largest or widest crater on the moon is Bailly, which is 303 km (188 miles) in diameter at its widest point of the rim.

STARS AND GALAXIES

LARGEST STAR

VY Canis Majoris is the largest known star. Canis Majoris means *big dog* in Latin. The star is red in appearance and is one of the brightest stars spotted so far. Found in the constellation Canis Major, VY Canis Majoris is about 5,000 light years away from Earth and one billion times bigger than the Sun in volume! It is 1,800–2,100 solar diameters across.

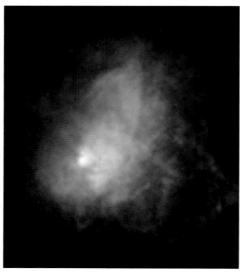
Visible light

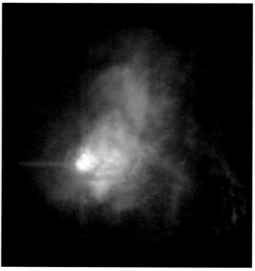
Polarised light

OLDEST STAR

HE0107-5240 is thought to date back about 14 billion years to the beginning of the universe. It came into existence after the Big Bang and is made of simple elements. Unlike younger stars, it contains almost no metal. HE0107-5240 is mostly made up of hydrogen, helium and lithium.

SMALLEST STAR

OGLE-TR-122b is the smallest known star, with a radius of about 0.12 solar radii. It is just 16 per cent larger than Jupiter, the biggest planet in our solar system, but is 96 times greater in mass. OGLE-TR-122b is actually a *red dwarf* star and belongs to the constellation known as Carina. This star crosses the star OGLE-TR-122 every 7 days 6 hours and 27 minutes. This decreases the light of OGLE-TR-122 reaching the Earth by 1.5 per cent. Scientists reasearched the cause for this and discovered a small star that they named OGLE-TR-122b, after the Optical Gravitational Lensing Experiment that was used.

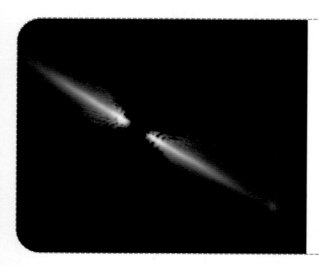

YOUNGEST STAR

AU Microscopium (AU Mic) is believed to be the youngest star. It is also one of the closest to Earth – just 33 light years away. About 12 millions years old, it is about half the mass of the Sun. It is an M-type star, which is considered the coolest. Currently, AU Mic is the subject of lots of research. Scientists are hoping to discover newly formed planets around it!

Did you know?

When a star exhausts itself of hydrogen, gravity takes over and the star explodes, forming a black hole. A black hole has such powerful gravity that it pulls everything into it — even light!

LARGEST GALAXY

Andromeda, or Messier 31, is the largest galaxy in the local group that contains about 35 galaxies including the Milky Way. Andromeda has a trillion stars and is about twice the size of the Milky Way. The spiral galaxy has a bright yellowish disk in the centre and bluish spiral arms.

HOTTEST STAR

The surface temperature of the bright white dwarf star NGC 2440 is more than 200,000 degrees Celsius (360,032 degrees Farenheit). It is so hot that it glows 250 times brighter than the Sun. The NGC 2440 is part of the Milky Way galaxy.

CLOSEST GALAXY

Canis Major Dwarf Galaxy is the closest galaxy to our Milky Way. It has a billion stars, of which a number are red giant stars. It is 25,000 light years from us and elliptical in shape.

MOST DETAILED IMAGE TAKEN OF A GALAXY

The Hubble Space Telescope's image of the Pinwheel Galaxy, or Messier 101 (M101) Galaxy, is the largest and most detailed photo of a spiral galaxy. One image is made up of 51 individual shots taken by the Hubble. The Pinwheel Galaxy is nearly twice the diameter of the Milky Way and holds about one trillion stars.

NEAREST STAR

The Sun is the closest star to the Earth. The next closest star is the Proxima Centauri, or Alpha Centauri C. This star is 4.3 light years from the Sun.

PLANETS

LARGEST PLANET

Jupiter, the fifth planet from the Sun, is the largest planet in our solar system. If all the other planets in the solar system were put together, Jupiter would still be two-and-a-half times larger! It is made up of 90 per cent hydrogen and 10 per cent helium. Although people knew of Jupiter in ancient times, Galileo Galilei was the first to study Jupiter through a telescope.

PLANET WITH THE SLOWEST ROTATION

Venus has the slowest rotation period among all the planets. One rotation of the planet takes 243 days. It also has a retrograde rotation, meaning that it rotates from east to west. Venus orbits the Sun once every 224.65 days, at an average distance of 68 million miles (108 million km). Venus comes closer to Earth than any other planet on its orbit. At its closest it is 24.9 million miles (40 million km) away.

HOTTEST PLANET

It is generally true that the closer a planet is to the Sun, the warmer it is. However, it is Venus, and not Mercury, which is the hottest planet in the solar system.
It is surrounded by a thick atmosphere which traps heat like a greenhouse. This thick blanket of atmosphere is mostly made up of carbon dioxide. The temperature on Venus is around 726 Kelvin (452 degrees Celsius or 870 degrees Fahrenheit). Venus is named after the Roman goddess of love.

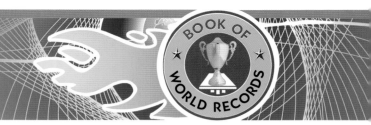

COLDEST PLANET

Neptune, named after the Roman god of the sea, is the eighth planet from the Sun. Neptune is the coldest planet in our solar system. The temperature here is around 48 Kelvin (-225 degrees Celsius or -373 degrees Fahrenheit). Neptune is a huge planet with a diameter of 30,778 miles (49,532 km), making it 3.88 times the diameter of Earth and the fourth largest planet after Jupiter, Saturn and Uranus. Neptune looks blue because of methane in its atmosphere.

Did you know?

Triton is the only moon in our solar system that orbits in the opposite direction to the direction of the planet it rotates around.

MOST MOONS

Jupiter has about 60 moons. Of these, the four largest moons are Io, Europa, Ganymede and Callisto. Metis is the moon closest to Jupiter. Saturn is second in the list with at least 33 moons, of which 18 have been named. Uranus is third with at least 18 moons.

SMALLEST PLANET

Mercury is the smallest planet in our solar system with a diameter of about 3,031 miles (4,878 km). Pockmarked with many craters, this rocky planet has no moon and no atmosphere. However, it does have a magnetic field. It is also the closest planet to the Sun and is visible from Earth at sunrise and sunset. Being closest to the Sun, Mercury is also the fastest planet in our solar system, taking just 88 days to complete one orbit!

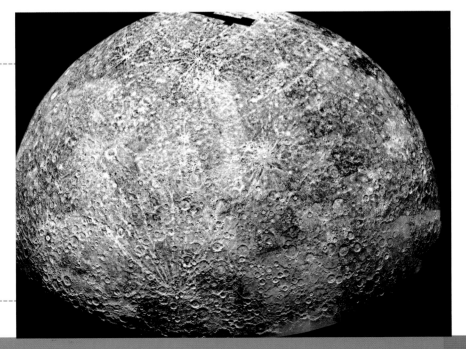

COMETS AND ASTEROIDS

MOST FAMOUS COMET

Halley's Comet gets its name from British astronomer Edmond Halley, who predicted that the comet would be seen every 75-76 years. The comet was first photographed in 1910. It is the only *short period comet*, or one that returns within a human lifetime and can be seen with the naked eye. It last appeared in 1986 and is expected to be visible from Earth again on July 28, 2061.

FIRST COMET OF THE 21ST CENTURY

Comet McNaught or C/2006 P1, the Great Comet of 2007, was discovered on August 7, 2006 by astronomer Robert H. McNaught. It was the brightest comet to be seen in 40 years, spotted in January and February 2007. It was so bright that on January 12, it could be seen even in daylight.

FIRST ASTEROID TO BE PHOTOGHAPHED

951 Gaspra was the first asteroid to be photographed in close-up, in 1991, by the spacecraft Galileo on its way to Jupiter. Photographs revealed that 951 Gapra had many small craters. Gaspra was discovered by Russian astronomer G. N. Neujmin in 1916. Galileo also photographed 243 Ida in 1993. The first asteroid probe was NEAR Shoemaker that took pictures of 253 Mathilde in 1997.

COMET WITH THE LONGEST TAIL

The comet Hyakutake has the longest tail among all comets that have been observed. Hyakutake has a bright, shining tail, over 354 million miles (570 million km) long. It was discovered by Yuji Hyakutake, a scientist from the UK, after whom the comet was named. The comet disappeared from sight on May 6, 1996. It is predicted that it will be 29,500 years before it reappears.

MOST OBSERVED COMET

Most comets are seen for just a matter of days. However, the comet Hale-Bopp, or C/1995 01, was visible to the naked eye from Earth for a full 18 months. Discovered on July 23, 1995, the comet was made popular by the then emerging technology of the Internet, where several sites charted the comet's progress and gave daily updates and images.

LARGEST ASTEROID

Ceres, spotted on January 1, 1801, was the first asteroid to be discovered. It is also the largest asteroid. The asteroid was discovered by Italian astronomer Giuseppe Piazzi who believed it was a planet. But in 1850, astronomers classified it as an asteroid. In 2006, Ceres was re-classified (along with Pluto) as a dwarf planet. Ceres, which lies between Mars and Jupiter, is about 578 miles (930 km) in diameter. This makes it the smallest dwarf planet in our solar system.

BRIGHTEST COMET

Discovered by Kaoru Ikeya and Tsutomu Seki, the comet Ikeya-Seki was first observed on September 18, 1965. It was so bright that it could be seen clearly, even during daylight, as it passed close to the Sun. The comet broke into three pieces as it passed close to the Sun and each piece continued in orbit. Ikeya-Seki is thought to be a fragment of a large comet that broke up in 1106 when it went too close to the Sun. Two of the fragments, S1-A and S1-B, will be seen from Earth in 2842 and 3021 respectively.

Did you know?

In the past, comets were named after the astronomers who found them. Now, they are labelled 'P' if they orbit the Sun more than once, or 'C' if they don't.

ONLY VISIBLE ASTEROID

Vesta, the brightest asteroid, is the only asteroid bright enough to be seen without a telescope. Vesta has a diameter of about 326 miles (525 km), and is the second largest asteroid. Vesta has a core of metal covered by a rocky crust. The asteroid was first discovered on March 29, 1807, by a German astronomer, Heinrich Olbers. Olbers had been searching for asteroids ever since the first asteroid , Ceres, was discovered accidentally in 1801. It was named by the German mathematician, Carl Gauss, after the Roman goddess of the home.

FIRST RECORDED COLLISION

The comet Shoemaker-Levy 9 was discovered in 1993 by astronomers Carolyn and Eugene Shoemaker and David Levy. It was seen in orbit around Jupiter in 1992. In July 1994, thousands of scientists watched in obsevatories around the world as the comet broke down into hundreds of pieces as it came close to Jupiter and dashed into its atmosphere. This was the first collision recorded between two objects in the solar system.

METEORS, METEORITES AND METEOROIDS

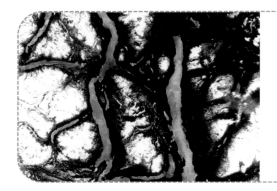

OLDEST METEORITE

A meteorite hit the Tagis Lake in Canada on January 18, 2000. More than 500 fragments of the meteoroite were collected. Each of the deep red-coloured pieces weighed about 1 kg (2.2 lbs). Careful research found that the meteorite was about 4.5 billion years old. The meteorite contained matter that existed before the solar system was even formed. This matter was a carbonaceous chondrite, containing organic compounds like amino acids – something that has been found in no other meteorite examined.

MYSTERY METEORITE

In 1916, Frenchman Captain Gaston Ripert claimed he had found an iron hill, 40 m (130 ft) high and 100 m (330 ft) wide, in Mauritania. Ripert claimed he was taken blindfolded to the iron hill, south-east of Chinguetti. From there he collected a 4 kg (8.8 lbs) fragment of rock to show to the world. Although the iron hill has never been found, the fragment was sent to Paris for analysis and scientists now believe that it was a meteor about 80 cm (31 in) in radius.

BIGGEST METEORITE

The Hoba meteorite is made of iron and landed in Namibia, Africa, about 80,000 years ago. It weighs about 54 tonnes (60 tons). It measures 2.7 m (8.9 ft) wide, 2.7 m (8.9 ft) long and 0.9 m (3 ft) high. It is the largest piece of natural iron in the world. Although it is so heavy, it did not form a larger crater probably because the Earth's atmosphere slowed it down.

METEORITE INJURY

There have been very few recorded instances of falling meteorites injuring people and animals, although the Valera meteorite did kill a cow. The first confirmed instance of a human being hit by a meteorite occurred on November 30, 1954, when an Ann Hodges of Alabama was hit by a 4 kg (8.8 lbs) stone chondrite that crashed into her living room through the roof. Hodges was badly bruised but made a full recovery.

Did you know?

Meteoroids have been known to have caused damage to spacecraft like the Hubble Space Telescope.

METEORITE ON MARS

Heat Shield Rock, later re-named Meridiani Planum, is an iron-nickel meteorite, found on Mars by the spacecraft *Opportunity* in January 2005. It got its first name because *Opportunity* found it near where it discarded its own heat shield. This was the first meteorite found on Mars.

LARGEST IMPACT CRATER

The largest verified crater caused by a meteorite on Earth is the Vredefort crater in South Africa. It is so large that a whole town, Vredefort, has grown in it. In 2005, it was included in the UNESCO World Heritage Site list. The crater is about 186 miles (300 km) across. It was created over two billion years ago and is the second oldest crater on Earth.

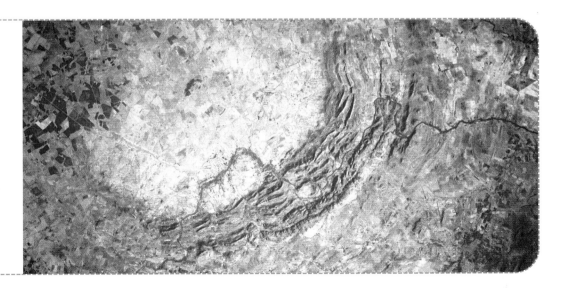

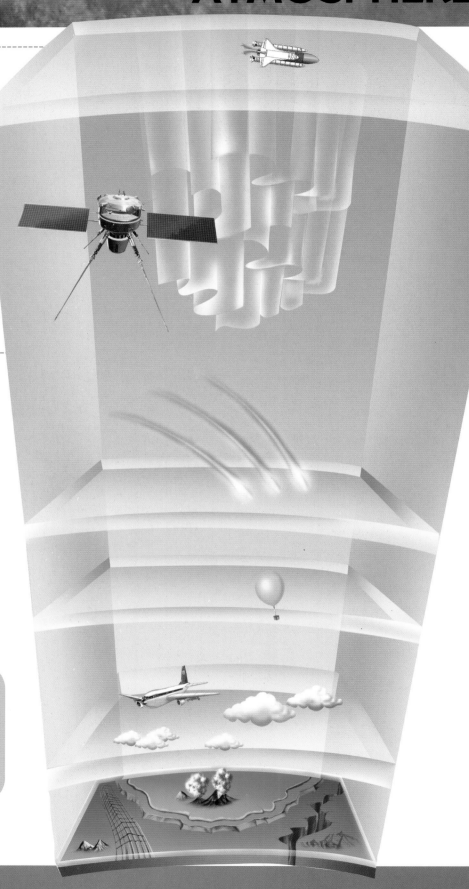

MOST DENSE LAYER OF ATMOSPHERE

The troposphere is the closest to Earth and is the lowest layer of the atmosphere. The troposphere is mostly made up of water vapour and extends up to 7.4 miles (12 km) from the Earth's surface. The troposphere is also the layer where there is weather and where clouds are formed. The troposphere gets its name from the Greek 'tropos', meaning mixing. Above this are the stratosphere, mesosphere, ionosphere, thermosphere and, finally, the exosphere.

HOTTEST LAYER OF ATMOSPHERE

The thermosphere gets its name from the Greek word 'thermos', meaning heat. As the name suggests, the thermosphere – which extends from about 50 miles (80 km) above the Earth's surface to about 398 miles (640 km) – is the hottest layer. It lies above the ionosphere and below the exosphere. The temperature of some gas particles here can rise to 2,000 degrees Celsius (3,632 degrees Fahrenheit)!

Did you know?

The atmosphere contains so much water that if it fell all at once as rain it could cover the entire surface of the Earth with 2.5 cm (1 in) of water.

LAYER WITH REVERSE TEMPERATURE

The stratosphere is the layer just above the troposphere and below the mesosphere, between 6 and 31 miles (10 and 50 km) from the Earth. The temperature in this layer is warmer than below and colder than above because the ultraviolet rays of the Sun heat the upper strata. The top of the stratosphere has a temperature of -3 degrees Celsius (26.6 degrees Fahrenheit), whereas the bottom is -60 degrees Celsius (-76 degrees Fahrenheit). Because of reduced wind turbulance, this is the height at which aircraft cruise.

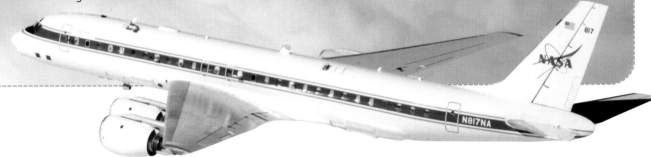

OUTERMOST LAYER

The exosphere is the outermost layer of the Earth's atmosphere. It extends from 311–621 miles (500-1000 km) above the Earth's surface and the upper boundary is at 6,214 miles (10,000 km). It is made up of light gases such as hydrogen, carbon dioxide and helium. Beyond the exosphere lies space.

LARGEST HOLE IN THE OZONE LAYER

The hole in the ozone layer over Antarctica measures more than 11 million sq/miles (28.3 million sq/km). Its size has been growing steadily since it was first spotted by British scientists in the 1970s. The ozone layer is like a blanket over the Earth's surface and absorbs harmful ultraviolet rays. The hole is caused by man-made gases like Chloroflurocarbons (CFCs), that were commonly used in refrigerators, aerosols and fire extinguishers before they were banned.

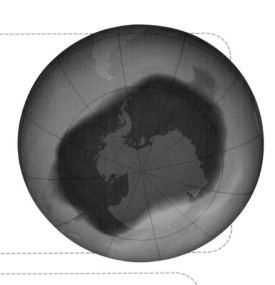

COLDEST LAYER

The mesosphere stretches from 31–50 miles (50-80 km) above the Earth. Temperatures in this layer are well below freezing and can fall as low as -100 degrees Celsius (-148 degrees Fahrenheit). This is also the layer where most meteoroids burn up after colliding with gas particles. Along with the stratosphere, the mesosphere forms the middle part of the atmosphere.

WILD WEATHER

RAINIEST PLACE

Mawsynram, in Meghalaya, India, is the wettest place in the world, with an average annual rainfall of 1,186 cm (467 in)! Mount Wai-'ale'ale on the island of Kauai, Hawaii has the most number of rainy days in a year. On average, it rains 350 days annually.

STRONGEST HURRICANE

Hurricane Wilma, which struck in October 2005, reached the highest recorded wind speed of 175 mph (281 km/h). It caused so much destruction that it was rated as one of worst hurricanes ever recorded. There were four fierce, or Category 5, hurricanes in 2005 — Emily, Katrina, Rita and Wilma. Combined, they caused more than 2,280 deaths and $128 billion of damage to property.

LARGEST HAILSTONE

On 22 June 2003 a hailstone 18 cm (7 in) in diameter and 48 cm (18.75 in) in circumference fell in Aurora in Nebraska, USA. One of the most expensive hailstorms hit St. Louis, USA on 10 April 2001. The unusually large hailstones damaged property worth $1.9 billion. The worst hailstorm in terms of human losses was recorded in the 9th century in Roopkund, India, which killed several hundred pilgrims.

GREATEST SNOWFALL

The most snowfall in one year was recorded in Mount Baker, USA, which is 3,284 meters (10,775 ft) above sea level. In 1998–99, Mount Baker witnessed 2,896 cm (1,140 in) of snowfall. The previous record of 2,850 cm (1,122 in) was set at the Rainier-Paradise National Weather Service Cooperative station during the 1971–72 season.

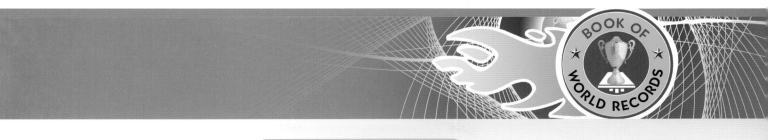

STRONGEST CYCLONE

On 12 November 1970 the strongest and deadliest cyclone ever recorded hit East Pakistan (now Bangladesh). The Bhola Cyclone was recorded as a Category 3 hurricane. Winds hit East Pakistan at 138 mph (222 km/h). About 500,000 people died and 100,000 people went missing. 3.6 million people were affected by the disaster. Those at sea did not escape: the freight ship, Mahajagmitra, sank in the storm killing all 50 people onboard.

Did you know?

The most damaging hurricane ever recorded was named Katrina. The hurricane formed during the 2005 Atlantic hurricane season and caused over $100 billion of damage to property.

LONGEST DRY SPELL

Arica, in Chile, suffered the longest recorded dry period of 14 years, lasting from October 1903 to January 1918!

WARMEST YEAR

The Earth's average temperature has warmed by about 0.8 degrees Celsius (1.4 degrees Fahrenheit) in the past century. 2005 was the hottest recorded year for more than a century. The previous warmest year waw recorded in 1988. 2002, 2003 and 2004 follow as the next three warmest years.

FLOODS AND FIRES

WORST FLOOD

The flooding of the Huang He, or Yellow River, China, in 1931, caused immense damage to life and property. At least 1 million people died, though some estimates place the total as high as 3.7 million. The Yellow River gets its name from the huge amount of silt that the river carries. This silt is vital to the fertility of the surrounding land. However, the silt deposits are also blamed for devastating flooding in lower lying regions.

MOST FLOOD-PRONE COUNTRY

Bangladesh is a low-lying country criss-crossed by about 150 rivers. Since its independence in 1971 it has suffered over 200 natural disasters, such as floods, cyclones, earthquakes and drought.

MOST WIDESPREAD FLOODING

The unusually heavy rainy season of 2007 caused floods across India, Nepal, Bangladesh and Bhutan. It left more than 2,000 people dead while more than twenty million people had to evacuate their homes. An unusually high amount of melting snow caused the River Brahmaputra to flood, while heavy rains and landslides caused even more damage.

WORST FIRE ON A PASSENGER SHIP

On December 21, 1987, the Doña Paz passenger ferry, travelling from Tacloban City, Philippines, to Leyte, Manila, collided with Vector, an oil tanker carrying 8,800 barrels of petroleum. The barrels caught fire and the fire spread to Doña Paz. The official death toll was 1,565, but the actual figure is believed to have been more than 4,000. Soon after the collision, the ferry sank.

WORST FACTORY FIRE

On May 10, 1993, a fire broke out in the Kader Toy Factory in Bangkok, Thailand. It took fire-fighters 40 minutes to reach the factory. By the time the fire was put out, at least 188 people had died while 500 others were injured.

WORST WILDFIRE

From October 8 to 14, 1871, a wildfire swept across Peshtigo, USA, killing 1,500 people and destroying four million acres. Peshtigo had been in the grip of a terrible drought and hot summer. At the time farmers were using the 'slash and burn' method of clearing forest land, which started many small fires. On the night of October 8, a storm blew the fire into an inferno.

Did you know?

Venezuela witnessed the worst flood in its history on December 15, 1999. Floods swept the country for a full week and left more than 10,000 people dead.

EARTHQUAKES

MOST POWERFUL EARTHQUAKE

On May 22, 1960, an earthquake measuring 9.5 on the Richter scale hit the southern coast of Chile and set off a powerful tsunami. The waves rose to 25 m (82 ft). More than 130,000 houses were destroyed and 2 million people were left homeless. The two disasters happened so fast that no one could estimate which one caused more deaths. About 2,290 lives were lost across the two disasters.

EARLIEST RECORDED EARTHQUAKE

The earliest record of an earthquake has been traced back to the year 1831 BC, when the Chinese recorded an earthquake that shook Shandong province of China. The account was carved into bamboo.

MOST DEADLY EARTHQUAKE

Around 830,000 people died in the earthquake that hit the Shaanxi province of China on January 23, 1556. The earthquake destroyed houses across an area of 520 sq/miles (837 sq/km). Most of the people lived in soft clay caves or 'yaodong', which collapsed, trapping their inhabitants. Scientists believe the earthquake measured 8 on the Richter scale. Even rivers changed course after the earthquake. Aftershocks from the quake were felt for six months. The earthquake also damaged the famous Small Wild Goose Pagoda, destroying the roof.

LONGEST FAULT CAUSED BY AN EARTHQUAKE

On December 26, 2004, a powerful earthquake hit Sumatra. This earthquake is believed to have caused a fault on the sea floor about 800 miles (1,287 km) long.

MOST DEVASTATING TSUNAMI

On December 26, 2004, a powerful, 9.3 magnitude, earthquake began under the sea off the coast of Sumatra. It set off a series of tsunamis that devastated large parts of Indonesia, Myanmar, Sri Lanka, Bangladesh, India, Thailand and even South Africa. Lasting around 10 minutes, it was the longest and second-most powerful earthquake ever recorded and the most powerful in the past 40 years. The entire Earth vibrated. It set off earthquakes in distant Alaska. This great earthquake was followed by another one — the third most powerful on record – just three months later on March 28, 2005.

VOLCANOES

LARGEST ACTIVE VOLCANO

Mauna Loa in Hawaii is the largest active volcano in the world. Its name means 'Long Mountain' in Hawaiian. It rises 4,169 m (13,679 ft) above sea level. It has the greatest volume of any volcano covering 18,000 cubic miles (75,027 cubic km). Mauna Loa has probably been active for the last 700,000 years. The last eruption was on March 24, 1984 and lasted until April 15, 1984.

DEADLIEST VOLCANO

Mount Tambora is an active volcano in Indonesia. It is 4,300 m (14,108 ft) high. It erupted in April 1815, killing more than 11,000 people directly, with 71,000 deaths in total attributed to the eruption. The explosion was so strong that it affected the climate in a large part of the world – so much so that the following year became known as the 'Year without a Summer'.

Did you know?

Formed near the eastern side of the Kilauea Volcano, Kazumura Cave in Hawaii is the deepest lava cave in the world. It is 38 miles (61.4 km) long and descends 1,099 m (3,605 ft).

HIGHEST VOLCANO

Ojos del Salado in Chile is 6,891 m (22,608 ft) tall — the highest in the world! Although it has not been truly active for at least 1,300 years, some ash found near the volcano suggests that there might have been some slight volcanic activity as recently as 1993. This volcano has two summits, with the Chilean summit higher than the Argentine summit by 1 m (3 ft). The border between the two countries passes between the peaks.

YOUNGEST VOLCANO

On February 20, 1943, a volcano grew out of a corn field in Mexico and, in one year, reached 336 m (1,102 ft) in height! In its first year, it buried the villages of Paricutin and San Juan Parangaricutiro in lava. The volcano erupted for nine years and it is now 424 m (1,391 ft) high.

TALLEST ACTIVE GEYSER

The Steamboat Geyser in Wyoming erupts to heights of about 100 m (328 ft). The eruptions can last for anything from 3 to 40 minutes although the geyser will then lie dormant for up to 50 years. The geyser has two vents about 5 m (16 ft) apart.

TALLEST GEYSER

Waimangu in New Zealand spurted water 457 m (1,500 ft) high. It last erupted between 1900 and 1904, throwing mud and rocks. It fell dormant in 1904 when the water table changed after a landslide.

LOUDEST EXPLOSION

The volcano on Krakatoa Island between Java and Sumatra has exploded many times. The explosion on August 26, 1883, hurled rocks 34 miles (55 km) into the air. The sound of its explosion was so loud that it could be heard on Rodrigues Island, near Mauritius, about 3,107 miles (5,000 km) away. More than 36,000 people died in the eruption and from the resulting tsunami that the volcano generated.

NATURAL RESOURCES

TALLEST GRANITE MONOLITH

El Capitan, in Yosemite National Park, USA, is 1,098 m (3,604 ft) tall. The rock is a part of the Sierra Nevada range. It got its name from the Mariposa Battalion which was in the region in 1851. Locally, the granite monolith is known as Totokonoolah.

LARGEST CONTINENT

Covering over 17.2 million sq/miles (44.3 million sq/km), Asia is the world's largest continent. It covers some 29.4 per cent of the Earth's total land area. Asia also has the largest population of any continent, with about four billion people living here. That's equivalent to more than 60 per cent of the world's total population!

RUSSIA
TURKEY
KAZAKHSTAN
MONGOLIA
JAPAN
IRAN
AFGHANISTAN
CHINA
SAUDI ARABIA
PAKISTAN
NEPAL
INDIA
PHILIPPINES
THAILAND
CAMBODIA
MALAYSIA
SINGAPORE

MOST COMMON ELEMENT

Hydrogen is the most common element found in the universe. It is also the lightest. It is colourless and odourless. Hydrogen is reactive and inflammable. Stars are made up of hydrogen. On Earth, oxygen is the most common element and helps us breathe and live.

HARDEST MINERAL

Diamond, an element of carbon, is the hardest natural material found on Earth. It is so hard that only another diamond or ultra-hard fullerite (a form of carbon harder than diamond) can scratch it. Diamond gets its name from the Greek word 'adamas', meaning something that cannot be conquered. The quality of a diamond is judged by the 'four Cs': carat, clarity, cut and colour. Most of the diamonds mined are found in Africa. The hardest diamonds are found in New England and New South Wales.

LARGEST CRYSTAL

A beryl found in Malakialina, Madagascar, measured 18 m (59 ft) long, 3.5 m (11.4 ft) in diameter and had a volume of 143 cubic/m (5,050 cubic/ft) and a mass of approximately 380,000 kg (419 tons)! Beryl is most commonly used as a gemstone. Pure beryls are colourless but most are tinted by impurities. They can be green, blue, yellow and red. Red beryl crystals are small and rare.

HIGHEST MOUNTAIN

Mount Everest is 8,848 m (29,029 ft) high and is famously the highest mountain the world! The mountain is part of the Mahalangur range of the Himalayas. On May 29, 1953, Sherpa Tenzing Norgay and Edmund Hillary became the first people to scale Everest's summit. Everest got its present name in 1865 from Colonel Sir George Everest, the Surveyor General of India.

HIGHEST MOUNTAIN RANGE ON LAND

The Himalayas, a mountain range in Asia, has some of the highest peaks in the world, including Mount Everest. It has a chain of more than 100 mountains that are higher than 7,200 m (23,622 ft). The range gets its name from the Sanskrit words for snow (hima) and home (alaya). The Himalayas span six countries — from Afghanistan in the west, through Pakistan, India, China, Nepal and Bhutan.

Did you know?

Mountains occur more often in oceans than on land. In fact, some of the islands in the world are nothing but the peaks of mountains coming out of the water.

LONGEST UNDERWATER MOUNTAIN RANGE

The Mid-Ocean Ridge runs underwater. It extends 40,000 miles (64,374 km) from the Arctic Ocean to the Atlantic Ocean. The ridge is created where tectonic plates overlap, the resulting friction driving magma upwards and splitting the ocean bed like a big crack.

DEEPEST DEPRESSION

The Marianas Trench is 7 miles (11 km) deep in the floor of the Pacific Ocean. The Challenger, a ship of the Royal Navy, sent the first expedition to survey the trench in 1951.

DEEPEST VALLEY

The Kali Ghandaki Gorge in Nepal is 6,400 m (20,997 ft) deep and 17 miles (28 km) wide. It is the deepest valley in the world. It separates Mount Annapurna (8,078 m (26,503 ft)) from Mount Dhaulagiri (8,172 m (26,811 ft)).

LONGEST MOUNTAIN RANGE ON LAND

The Andes mountain range in South America stretches over 4,500 miles (7,242 km) in length and 500 km (311 miles) in width. Its highest peak is Aconcagua, which rises to 6,962 m (22,841 ft) above sea level. The Andes are more than twice the width of the Himalayas.

PLATEAUS AND RIDGES

LARGEST DISSECTED PLATEAU

Plateaus that are uplifted by the movement of the Earth's tectonic plates and then eroded by wind and water are called dissected plateaus. The Cumberland, or Allegheny, Plateau, west of the Appalachian Mountains, is cut into many gorges and cliffs. The extent of the dissected plateau is illustrated on the map in dark green.

HIGHEST PLATEAU

Known as the roof of the world, the Tibetan Plateau is the highest and biggest plateau in the world. The plateau is 1,553 miles (2,500 km) long and 621 miles (1,000 km) wide and is about 4,500 m (14,764 ft) above sea level. The plateau gets about 10-30 cm (4-12 in) of rain and over 30 days of hailstorms a year. Major rivers like the Indus, Satluj, Tsangpo, Mekong, Yangtse, Haung Ho and the Irrawaddy begin here.

SECOND-HIGHEST PLATEAU

Altiplano, which means 'High Plain' in Spanish, lies in the Central Andes in South America. It rises to 4,000 m (13,123 ft) above sea level. Lake Titicaca sits on this plateau and is the highest commercially navigable lake in the world. To the south of the Altiplano lies the Atacama Desert, the driest region on Earth. Parts of it are so dry that the soil looks red, giving it an almost martian appearance in places.

HIGHEST RIDGE IN THE WORLD

The Pyynikki Ridge in the city of Tampere, Finland, is part of a line of ridges that run from Kankaanpää to Salpausselkä. Of these ridges, Pyynikki is the highest gravel ridge in the world. Formed about 10,000 years ago during the Ice Age, the ridge lies 162 m (531 ft) above sea level and comprises of a moraine ridge and bedrock that date back to much before the Ice Age.

DEEPEST CANYON

The Yarlung Tsangpo canyon in Tibet is considered to be the deepest canyon in the world. The canyon is 5,075 m (16,650 ft) deep. This canyon also encloses the peaks of Namche Barwa (7,753 m (25,436 ft)) and Jala Peri (7,282 m (23,891 ft)). The Yarlung Tsangpo River flows between them at an elevation of 2,438 m (8,000 ft).

Did you know?

A plateau is different from a mountain in that a mountain has a jagged peak while a plateau has a flat top. A plateau is formed either when mountains get worn down or when large portions of flat earth are pushed up.

LOWEST VALLEY

Death Valley in California and Nevada, USA, is 86 m (282 ft) below sea level. While temperatures fall to below freezing in winter, they can rise as high as 54 degrees Celsius (130 degrees Fahrenheit) in summer. The lowest point in the valley is Badwater.

NULLARBOR PLAIN
WESTERN END OF TREELESS PLAIN

LARGEST LIMESTONE PLAINS

The Nullarbor Plain covers 77,200 sq/miles (20,000 sq/km) in Western and Southern Australia. The name Nullarbor means 'no trees'. While the plain has no major trees, it is covered with bluebush and saltbush plants, as well as acacia and shrubs. The Australian aborigines call it 'Oondiri', or the waterless place. It gets about 20 cm (7.8 in) of rain every year. There are almost 800 species of plants and 250 bird species there.

Did you know?

Not all plains are found on land. Plains are also found on ocean beds. These are known as Abyssal plains and are some of the flattest and smoothest areas of the world.

LARGEST UNBROKEN LOWLAND

The West Siberian Plain stretches from the Ural mountains in the west to the Yenisi River in the east in Siberia – from the Arctic Ocean in the north to the Altay Mountains in the south. It covers 1.6 million sq/miles (2.7 million sq/km) – a third of Siberia! More than 50 per cent of the plain is less than 101 m (330 ft) above sea level.

DEEPEST VALLEY

Owens Valley in south-east California, USA, is 75 miles (120 km) long. The valley is as deep as 1,200 m (4,000 ft) in places! To its west is Sierra Nevada. On the east are the White Mountains.

LARGEST U-SHAPED CANYON

The Yarlung Zangbo River, which flows through Tibet, has carved out the world's largest U-shaped canyon, around the Namjagbarwa peak in the eastern part of the Himalayas. The canyon is 313.5 miles (504.6 km) long and its average depth is 2,268 m (7,441 feet). At its deepest point the canyon descends to 6,009 m (19,714 ft)!

MOST POPULATED PLAIN

The Indo-Gangetic plain covers most of northern India, all of Bangladesh and some of Pakistan. It is a plain drained by the Ganga and Indus rivers. The land around these two river systems is home to about 900 million people!

FORESTS AND DESERTS

LARGEST RAINFOREST

The Amazon rainforest covers over 3.4 million sq/miles (5.5 million sq/km). Such is its size, it spreads across nine countries in South America, with the majority (60 per cent) lying in Brazil. The rainforest represents more than half of all the remaining rainforest in the world! The Amazon is exceptional in its biodiversity. Indeed, more than one-third of all animal species are found here. The greatest threat to the Amazon rainforest is deforestation, with humans clearing huge areas of forest for agriculture and wood.

MOST FORESTED COUNTRY

Although Brazil contains 60 per cent of the Amazon rainforest, covering some 2.1 million sq/miles (5.4 million sq/km) of forests, it is Russia that tops the list with 3.3 million sq/miles (8.5 million sq/km) of forests! This equates to about 22 per cent of the total forest cover in the world. If all the forests of Russia were put together, the area would be greater than the USA! Most of these forests are coniferous.

Did you know?

The Sonoran Desert in North America has the richest diversity of plants and animals of any desert in the world. It is also considered the wettest desert in the world.

LARGEST ICE DESERT

Antarctica covers 5.5 million sq/miles (14.2 million sq/km). Antarctica gets less than 5 cm (2 in) of rain annually. It is the southernmost continent, with 98 per cent of its area covered with ice at an an average thickness of 1.6 km (1 mile)! It is the driest, windiest and coldest continent in the world. Temperatures here can fall to -90 degrees Celsius (-130 degrees Fahrenheit) in winter!

LARGEST HOT DESERT

The Sahara Desert in North Africa covers 3.5 million sq/miles (9 million sq/km). This is greater than the landmass of Australia! It stretches across several countries, including Algeria, Chad, Egypt, Burkina Faso, Mali, Niger, Mauritania, Senegal, Libya, Sudan and Tunisia. The Nile and Senegal rivers flow through it.

DRIEST DESERT

The Atacama of Chile is the driest desert in the world. Parts of it have not received rain in 20 million years. In 1971, rain fell on some parts of the desert for he first time in 400 years. The desert is locked between two mountain ranges, which blocks rainfall from both sides.

SEAS AND OCEANS

LARGEST OCEAN

Named by Portuguese explorer Ferdinand Magellan, the Pacific Ocean occupies roughly one-third of the Earth's surface. It stretches 65.3 million sq/miles (169.2 million sq/km) from the Arctic to the Antarctic, between Asia and Australia on one side and the Americas, on the other. The Atlantic Ocean is the second largest on Earth after the Pacific Ocean.

Did you know?

The Pacific Ocean covers 32% of the Earth and 46% of its water surface. This is more than the area covered by land on Earth.

SHALLOWEST SEA

A section of the Black Sea, the Sea of Azov, is the shallowest sea in the world, with a depth of just 14.5 m (47 ft). Some portions of it measure less than 1 m (3.2 ft) in depth. It is 211 miles (340 km) long and 84 miles (135 km) wide. Located to the north of the Black Sea, it is connected to it by the Strait of Kerch. On one side of it lies Russia, and on the other, the Ukraine. The rivers Kuban and Don flow into it.

DEEPEST BLUE HOLE

A blue hole is created when rainwater soaks through limestone. Blue holes are about 15,000 years old with most of them measuring about 110 m (360 ft) in depth. Dean's blue hole on Long Island, Bahamas, is recorded as the deepest blue hole in the world. It is 202 m (663 ft) deep, almost round in shape and has a diameter of 25–35 m (82-115 ft).

SMALLEST OCEAN

The Arctic Ocean in the northern hemisphere is the smallest and shallowest of the world's five major oceans. It occupies a roughly circular basin and covers an area of 5.4 million sq/miles (14 million sq/km). The ocean is virtually landlocked and is surrounded by Greenland, North America and Eurasia. It is connected to the Pacific Ocean by the Bering Strait. The Arctic Ocean has a large covering of sea ice for most of the year.

LARGEST SEA

The South China Sea is a part of the Pacific Ocean. It covers 1.3 million sq/miles (3.5 million sq/km). Several rivers, including the Mekong, Min, Pearl and Rajang, flow into the sea. The sea touches China, Hong Kong, Taiwan, the Philippines, Macao, Singapore, Thailand, Cambodia, Vietnam and Taiwan.

LARGEST BAY

Hudson Bay – named after Henry Hudson who explored the bay in 1610 aboard his ship, Discovery – lies in north-east Canada. It is about 1.23 million sq/km in area and is connected to the Atlantic Ocean by the Hudson Strait. To the north it connects with the Arctic Ocean. It is ice covered for much of the year.

LONGEST RIVER

Some 4,160 miles (6,695 km) long, the Nile is the longest river in the world. It flows north through Africa into the Mediterranean Sea. The Nile and its tributaries flow through several countries, including the Democratic Republic of Congo, Egypt, Ethiopia, Eritrea, Kenya, Sudan, Uganda, Tanzania, Rwanda and Burundi. Its two major tributaries are the White Nile and the Blue Nile.

HIGHEST RIVER

The Dudh Kosi, which begins on Mount Everest, is the highest river in the world. The river is created by the melting Khumbu glacier at 5,334 m (17,500 ft). It is a fast-moving river and is dotted with frequent waterfalls and whirlpools. It joins the Sun Kosi River near Harkapur in Nepal to form the river Kosi.

DEEPEST RIVER

The River Sepik, in Papua New Guinea, is 20 m (66 ft) deep in places and more than 200 m (656 ft) deep at the mouth where it meets the Bismarck Sea.

LARGEST ESTUARY

An estuary is the end of the river where it meets the sea. A river is usually widest at its estuary. Chesapeake Bay in the USA carries the water of more than 50 major and minor rivers. It is about 200 miles (322 km) long and even at its narrowest point it is 4 miles (6 km) wide. At its widest point – where the Potomac River flows into it – the estuary is 30 miles (50 km) across. The bay stretches from the Susquehanna River in the north to the Atlantic Ocean in the south.

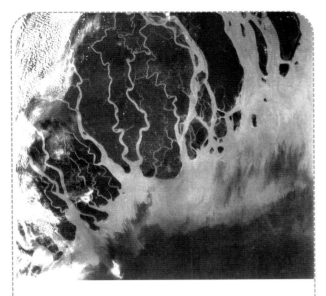

LARGEST DELTA

A delta is the mouth of a river, where it meets the sea. It is usually triangular in shape. The Ganga delta in the Indian sub-continent covers parts of India and Bangladesh and empties into the Bay of Bengal. It is about 220 miles (350 km) long and covers an area of more than 40,790 sq/miles (105,645 sq/km). Several major rivers including the Padma, Meghna and Jamuna flow into it.

LARGEST RIVER

The Amazon is the largest river in the world in terms of the volume of water it carries to the sea. In fact, the river accounts for one-fifth of the world's total river flow! The Amazon flows through South America and its many tributaries cut through the Amazon rainforest, helping to give life to a large variety of flora and fauna. The river is so voluminous that it is often called 'the River Sea'. It also has the world's largest river basin. In 2007, researchers claimed to have found a new source of the Amazon in the frozen Mismi mountain in South Peru at a height of 5,000 m (16,404 ft). If proven, that would make the Amazon 4,225 miles (6,800 km) long (and longer than the Nile)!

Did you know?

The Amazon River is the widest river in the world. It stretches 28 miles (45 km) across in places during the rainy season. It starts as a small stream in the mountains of Peru and is so vast that no bridge crosses it.

LARGEST FRESHWATER LAKE (BY VOLUME)

Lake Baikal in southern Russia holds more water than any other freshwater lake. It contains about 5,521 cubic/miles (23,000 cubic/km) of water. This is about one-fifth of all the freshwater on the Earth's surface! This slim, long, crescent-shaped water body is also considered to be the deepest lake in the world. It is 1,637 m (5,371 ft) deep and the water rests on about 4.3 miles (7 km) of sediment.

VASTEST LAKE

The Caspian Sea is a salt water lake because it is completely surrounded by land. It covers some 143,244 sq/miles (371,000 sq/km) and holds 18,761 cubic/miles (78,200 cubic/km) of water. The Caspian Sea is 1,025 m (3,363 ft) deep. The roughly bean-shaped sea lies between the Russian Federation and Iran and also touches Kazakhstan, Turkmenistan and Azerbaijan. It contains salt water because it was once a part of the ancient Tethys Sea.

HIGHEST NAVIGABLE LAKE

Lake Titicaca lies 3,812 m (12,507 ft) above sea level. The lake is in the Andes Mountains, between Bolivia and Peru. It is also the largest lake in South America. The lake is made up of two nearly-separate water bodies connected by the Strait of Tiquina. It gets its water from glaciers and rain. At the deepest point, it measures 284 m (932 ft). By volume, the lake is the largest in South America.

LARGEST RESERVOIR

The largest artificial lake in the world is Lake Volta in Ghana. It was created when the Akosombo Dam was constructed in 1965. The lake covers a vast area of some 3,283 cubic/miles (8,502 cubic/km)!

Did you know?

Lake Nyos in Cameroon is the deadliest lake in the world. It contains toxic gases which have caused about 2,000 deaths in recent times.

HIGHEST LAKE

The Lhagba Pool, on the north-east slope of Mount Everest in Tibet, is 6,368 m (20,892 ft) above sea level and is currently the highest lake in the world. However, a lake in a crater has recently been discovered on the eastern side of Ojos del Salado, the highest volcano in the world. The lake is at a height of 6,390 m (20,965 ft) but is yet to be named. The lake is about 100 m (300 ft) in diameter. Once named, it will be recognised as the highest lake.

TALLEST STALAGMITE

The Zhi Jin Cave, in China, has a stalagmite that is 70 m (230 ft) high. Around it are several other stalagmites that measure up to 40 m (131 ft) in height. The cave itself is 7 miles (12 km) long with huge passages and chambers. The Cueva San Martin Infierno cave in Cuba has the second tallest stalagmite in the world. It is 67.2 m (220 ft) high.

LONGEST STALACTITE

About 518 m (1,700 ft) into the cave of Sistema Chac Mol, Mexico, is a large room about 27 m (90 ft) deep. In the centre of the room is the Xich Ha Tunich, or the Giant Drip Stone stalactite — the longest in the world! This wonder of nature attracts many tourists each year.

DEEPEST CAVE

Explorers are still discovering new caves and they continue to find deep caves with every expedition. Currently, Voronya Pestera is the deepest cave to have been discovered so far. In October 2005, explorers of the CAVEX team confirmed that the depth of the cave is 2,190 m (7,185 ft). The cave lies in the western Caucasus region in Abkhazia, Georgia. The deepest point in the cave is under water and was only reached when a Czech explorer dived with breathing apparatus in February 2007.

LONGEST UNDERWATER CAVE

Sistema Ox Bel Ha, in Quintana Roo, Mexico, is the longest underwater cave system ever found. The cave has been mapped to a length of 83 miles (134 km) so far, making it the ninth longest cave system in the world. The next largest underwater cave is the Sistema Sac Actun, which is 38 miles (62 km) long and is also in Mexico.

THE BIGGEST CAVE CHAMBER

The Sarawak chamber – in the Lubang Nasib Bagus Cave, on the island of Borneo – is the world's largest unsupported underground cave chamber. It is around 700 m (2,296 ft) long, 450 m (1,476 ft) wide and over 70 m (230 ft) high. It is found in the Gunung Mulu National Park in Malaysia. This massive chamber would be able to hold as many as 8 Boeing 747 aircrafts!

LARGEST CAVE

Cheve Cave, in Mexico's Sierra de Juárez, has tunnels that run deeper than 2,000 m (6,500 ft). Krubera Cave, in the Republic of Georgia, comes second with tunnels that extend for 1,710 m (5,610 ft).

Did you know?

Goliath, part of the Cathedral Caverns in Grant, Alabama, is the world's widest stalagmite. It is 74 m (243 ft) in circumference at its base.

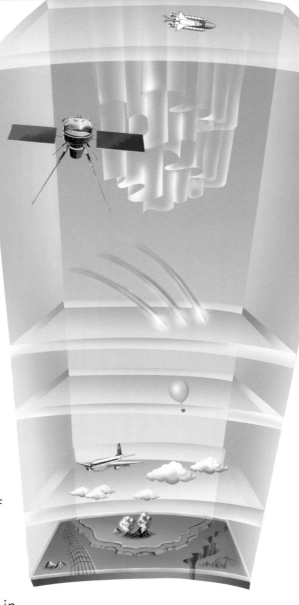

Ascend: To move upwards

Collision: To crash into something

Comet: An object in space made of ice and dust that emits a tail of gas when close to the sun

Constellation: A cluster of stars forming a recognisable pattern

Cyclone: A violent, rotating storm

Discard: To get rid of

Dromedaries: Member of the camel family

Emit: To let out

Fault: A fracture created in a rock formation due to an earthquake

Galaxy: A group of millions of stars travelling around is space, held together by a gravitational attraction

Geyser: A natural spring that lets out hot water and steam

Kelvin: A unit for measuring temperature. 1 K is equivalent to –272 degrees Celsius

Light year: A unit of measuring distance in space. 1 light year = 9.461×10^{12} km

Meteor: A small body of matter in the solar system that burns up when it enters the Earth's atmosphere

Meteorite: A portion of meteoroid that survives its passage through the Earth's atmosphere

Meteoroid: A small body of matter moving about in the solar system

Oblong: Elongated shape

Originate: To begin from

Sand dunes: Hills made of sand

Stalactite: A mineral that hangs from the ceiling of limestone caves

Stalagmite: A mineral that rises from the floor of limestone caves

Telescope: An instrument used to observe objects far away

Tsunami: A series of violent and huge waves created by an underwater earthquake or volcano

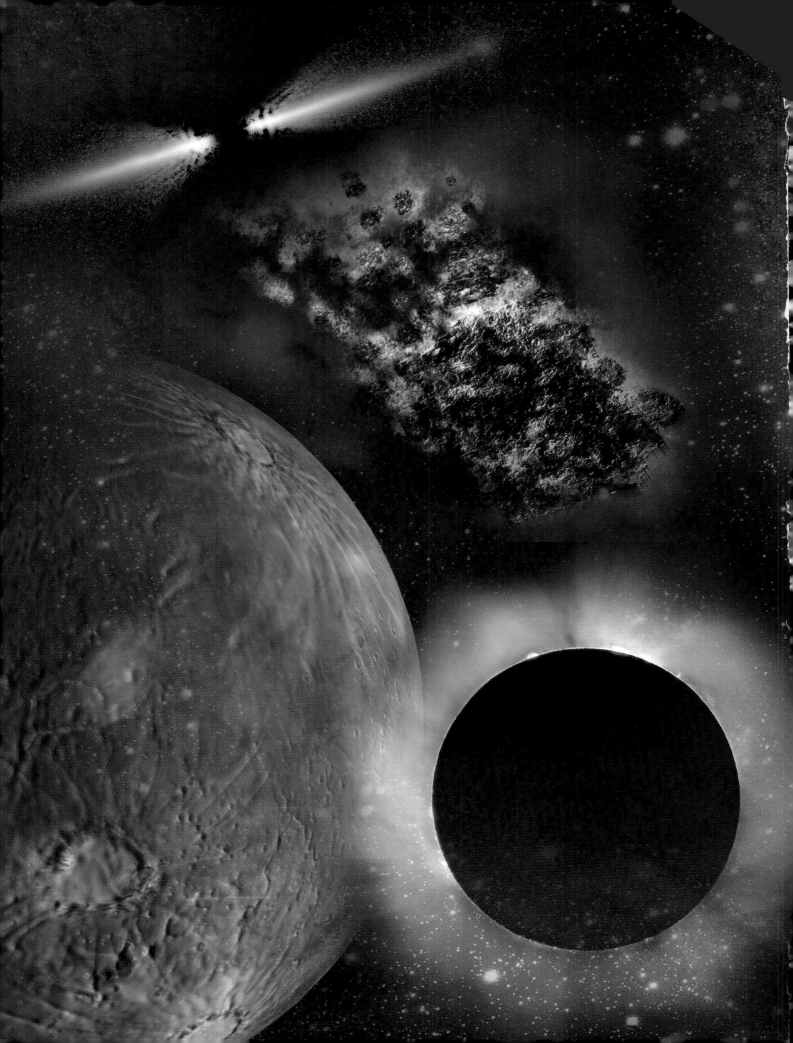